Gordon Damon

Poems of a Youthful Bard

Gordon Damon

Poems of a Youthful Bard

ISBN/EAN: 9783337329174

Printed in Europe, USA, Canada, Australia, Japan

Cover: Foto ©Thomas Meinert / pixelio.de

More available books at **www.hansebooks.com**

POEMS

OF

A YOUTHFUL BARD

WITH PREFATORY AND
EXPLANATORY NOTES

BY

AUTHOR

"Truth, Magnanimity, Perfection."

PHILADELPHIA
PRINTED BY J. B. LIPPINCOTT COMPANY

OUT OF RESPECT FOR AND APPRECIATION OF
HIS PATERNAL LOVE,

AND

FOR HIS AID

IN

PROCURING THE PUBLICATION OF THIS,

MY FIRST WORK,

IS THE SAME MOST SINCERELY

Dedicated

TO

MY FATHER.

CONTENTS.

9

PREFACE.

THE present volume is a compilation of a collection of youthful poems of "school-boy" days, composed in my fifteenth year,—1895. They are, for the most part, the results of study of and communion with external nature. In them I strive to bring out the love, the beauty, the grandeur, and even the intellect (?) characteristic of this queen of queens; this goddess administering to the wants of a tired earth; caressing it, and invoking a blessing on its welfare.

To me there is something distinct, apart from the inanimate in external nature. There is something human and divine. What wonder that some of the ancient peoples worshipped her forms? Surely, God inspires them with life, and has placed His image in them. I think she should be addressed and reverenced even as are the distinguished personages of this plain. We should search for her truths in the deep-delved earth; in the remote and obscure recesses of the woods and rocks,—

" Find tongues in trees, books in the running brooks,
Sermons in stones, and good in everything."

In placing the work before the public, I wish to ask its pardon; and when struck with the inconsistency and un-

11

ripeness, as may occur frequently, to bear in mind the conditions and the author.

As to "The Bird's Obituary," you must excuse me for writing on so trivial affairs. Byron has said,—

> "The puny school-boy and his early lay
> Men pardon if his follies pass away."

In the poems I have aimed towards originality; but, of course, as all authors have done, and probably always will, I have received ideas from other works, although I trust word-for-word quotations are infrequent. Plagiarism is a thing to be avoided. I think I have brought out something new; my friends are to vouch for it.

> "Read not to contradict and confute;
> . . . but to weigh and consider."

This volume may be subject to severe criticism, and it may not. Whatever be the case, the result will only serve as an incentive to a nobler object.

It may not receive the public favor. Byron, Shelley, Keats, Wordsworth, and a host of others, met with opposition and discouragement in their early years, but did that check their progress? Keats, although conceded to be an inferior and youthful writer, has promise in his works. There is promise in them which seems to portend the greatness of the soul back of it; and, had his life been spared, he would have doubtless astonished the world with his sensuousness.

Sometimes "a sharp criticism that has a drop of witty

venom in it stings a young author almost to death," but
if this volume meets with such, providing it is worth criti-
cising, I will do my best to survive. Braveness and magnanimity (that property which enables one " to encounter
danger and trouble with tranquillity and firmness, which
raises the possessor above revenge and prompts him to act
and sacrifice for noble objects") are things invaluable in
this world. Byron was brave when he attacked the
"Scotch Reviewers," but his was braveness with malice
in it; braveness of hostility; braveness without magnanimity. "Calamity is man's true touchstone;" or, in
other words, the first failure is the first step to success.
How often has this been demonstrated !

In conclusion, I am sure my friends will find nothing in
the poems either impure or debasing. I trust the thought
in every case descends no lower than nobility. Wordsworth has wisely said,—

> " Learn by a mortal yearning to ascend
> Toward a higher object."

This expresses an ideal. That object is perfection.
And as this volume passes out of the press with all its
faults and all its gems (?), I promise you something better
in the future.

Respectfully yours,

GORDON A. DAMON.

MILLINGTON, MICHIGAN, July 8, 1895.

INTRODUCTORY .NOTE.

WE look forward to a future "Golden Age," as it were; to an age of peace, happiness, and contentment; to an age when there will be something in reality to live for other than individual supremacy; to an age when strife in all its various branches shall be obliterated, when mankind shall enjoy the highest good, and realize heaven upon the earth. We, no doubt, will not see it, but we trust posterity will. Can we not do otherwise than merely deem this age a myth of the past? When man's intellect is sufficiently developed and his eyes are open to the proper light of things, then shall he realize the change.

"Fantasia" is thoroughly a child of fancy.

POEMS

OF

A YOUTHFUL BARD.

FANTASIA: A VISION OF THE FUTURE.

PART I.

BLUE skies in glory beamed above,
And clouds, the breath of summer, decked
The vault thus formed with silver seas,
Which glistened as the sun shone through
The rifts and ripples of its morning tide.
A breeze bestirred itself that morn,
And as it passed o'er blooming fields
And meadows, pleasant lakes and streams,
It gathered in its bosom breath
Of flowers, elysian born, which bowed
Their heads in reverence to the God
Who made them, and who gave them grace
To cheer the hearts of mortals here below.

A cataract, hard by, sent up
A tune to heaven as it moved
O'er rocks and crags, and thundered down
The steep, with Nature as its guide,
Who led the way through curious rocks
And deep ravines, and through the caves
And crevices along its path.
Now here, now there, now darting to
And fro as if in play, but on
And on forever to the sea;
To sink into its bosom, thence
To rise unseen, and seek once more
The cataract from whence it sprung;
To fall, but soon to rise again.
The trees, the shrubs, the scandent stems,
And herbs sent up a vigorous growth,
And graced a landscape, which, in blend
And form, surpassed by far, of art,
The instruments and skill which man e'er caught,
And put to flight his puny masterpiece.
And emulous nature all around,
Beast, bird and insect,—all the forms
Of life,—anon put forth their best
In effort to succeed and bring forth joy.
Alburnus rested neath an elm

That, in the wisdom of its growth,
Had spread itself abroad and formed
A blest retreat from weary hours
Of toil.   Here oft he sat and lisped
Unto himself the thoughts that rushed
In quick succession through his brain ;
But on this morn of brighter mood
He seemed, and wandering far away
Were all his thoughts ; and as the breeze
Came stealing o'er his verdurous couch,
Bearing its fragrant burthen in its breast ;
And as he gazed upon the sky
And silvery clouds above, he seemed
To fade away : then, lulled to rest,
And charmed by aerial scenes, to be
Absorbed, and soon fell fast asleep.

PART II.

Now o'er the landscape changeling sped
His spirit free, and o'er the verge
To dreamland.   On he sped until
He wandered in elysium,
Among interminable paths and tufts
Of emerald.   Beauties greeted him

Which, to the mortal eye so gross,
Were inconceivable.   On he passed
In sweetest meditation.   Thoughts
Of future ages wandered each
O'er each in blest profusion through
His new-born, heavenly intellect.
Inspired !   The very thoughts put on
New forms,—anon uprose before
His transfixed gaze stupendous forms,
And towers of adamant, and vast
Arenas bearing crimson lengths,
Which hung as veils encircling all.

Colossus, like Alburnus, stood
Immovable in the maze around.
He gazed, but still perplexed,—o'ercome
With charms so striking, yet unsought.
    As thus he stood, there seemed a voice
From out the vaporous clouds to say,—
"Go forth, Alburnus.   Stay not here
And waste thy precious hours in gaze
And idleness ; but haste thee, haste
To that mysterious realm, and seek
Thy wisdom in its garnished halls
And o'er its plains ; haste, haste thee, son."

Bestirred Alburnus when the voice
Had ceased, and then with hastened step
Moved on the scene anon,—
Advanced, and thus addressed the Queen,—

"Oh, thou mysterious Future, in thy realms
Of unborn glories, hidden force and power,
Phenomena, which, man's prophecy, o'er-
    whelms,
And vast achievements,—meek Ambition's
    tower,—
        Oh, lift thy veil.

"Aye, condescend to lead me through thy ways,
And teach me all the wisdom thou must know;
Oh, guide me, teach me, and thy sight repays
My yearnings, as the lover to the beau
        Doth satisfy.

"Lift, lift the shroud that now surrounds, ob-
    scures thee,
And satisfy mine hungering soul with lore.
Mine eyes, oh, look, and penetrate the sea
Of crimson thou dost now behold,—adore,
        And lead me on."

Vanished the curtains, and his sight
Beheld the spectacle of his dream,—
Her Majesty, clad in robes the breath
Of gold, the essence of its worth,
Who stood as guardian o'er the realm
And o'er the fancy of her guest.
He spake not, more,—the Queen had heard ;
He read the answer in her eye ;
His heart enthralled, the sight o'ercome,
He scarce could wait the Queen's reply,—
" Welcome, thou changeling ; follow me."
As doth the magnet rule the steel
So didst the Queen Alburnus rule ;
So didst her bearing catch his mind,
And drew his feet anon with her.

Behold !   Oh, what doth greet him now ?
What wondrous forms !   What shapely forms !
What genius blazoned all around !
What cressets of ingenious lore !
What superhuman feats entombed
In human casements !   Strength and power
Of mighty rulers yet unborn !
What sights and mysteries unfold !
Now musing pensively, and now

Casting his wanton eye abroad,
Alburnus, conscious of the Queen
And conscious of the state, exclaimed,—
" How wonderful are the works of God !
And man, the noblest in the scale,
How lofty his ambition, and
How stern the motives of the soul !"
" O God, didst thou inspire these works?
Was't with thy skill he wrought the stone?
Is't with thy power such massive forms
Rise up before the startled morn ?" *
Now on the right and on the left
Great halls burst forth,—arched entrances,
To coy the child † and lead him on.
He moved.   What alien marvels rear ! ‡
Here sits stern Justice on the throne.
Here Education crowns each head.
Here Science thrives, and Wisdom fraughts

---

* Startled morn is a metaphor used to express the brilliancy with which the sun is supposed to have burst forth
and sent its rays over the landscape in streams of liquid
gold.

† His intellect was as a child's in this new realm.

‡ Rear in this position means a springing up, a springing
into existence.

All civil * hearts, and sends the waves
Of thought throughout the public air.
Here Argon and the electrics fade,
And give the place to higher forms.
Here stately vehicles relieve
The breath of horses past and gone.
Now fade the implements of war.
No bloody strife infects the creeds.
No party contest marks the years.
No ignorance, no theft, no vice,
No vile submission of the poor,
But all in one "harmonious whole,"—
The brotherhood of man,—the age
Of wealth, of reason, and of lore.

Dimly yet surely through the arch
Of tangled vistas shines a star,
The cynosure of all.   He moved,
And hastened more each step, each pace.
"Perfection!   Ah, deceitful star!
Thou *ignis fatuus* of the realms!
Canst thou not hold for man's desires?

---

* Civil hearts refers to men in the service of the country, the government; really, a politician. *Hearts* is a metonymy.

Wilt thou not now receive his prayer?"
Alburnus mused.   Now faint, now light,
Then bursting forth in one vast glare,
The beams o'erpowered his manly frame,—
Awoke his fancy with a start.
" O God," he said, " grant me once more
A sight of the future ; grant, oh, grant.
Perfection, ever in the eye,
Anon remains the thing before.
Man strives in vain to reach its heights,
But falls ere he has scaled the top."

POSTSCRIPT.

Thus on a time Alburnus, 'neath the elm,
Dreamt of the Future and its wondrous forms.
Now oft he strays to that same cosy spot,
To seek once more a vision of the realms,
But all to naught.   Hope " never spreads her
          wings ;"
'Tis action brings the soul its highest bliss.*

June, 1895.

* Hoping for that age is of no avail.

HYMN TO MUSIC.*

Come, holy mother, come and cheer thy son ;
   And from thy founts of pure delight and love,
   In thine eternal resting-place above,
Pour forth a draught of pleasure thou hast
    won.

Stir old Timotheus with thy magic hand ;
   Attune his lyre to move one's inmost soul ;
   Present thy choir, for we will ask no toll ;
Proclaim the nation's peace throughout the
    land.

Come from thy haunts wherein such pleasure
    lies ;
   Set me afloat upon elysian seas,
   And cease not till mine hung'ring doth ap-
    pease ;
Oh ! fill my soul with thine own rhapsodies.

---

* This was written while in a melancholy mood, and at
a time when out of music study.—AUTHOR.

TO A BIRD IN A CAGE.

First published poem.

Oh, prisoner, in behind those slender bars
Of ductile steel, inclosed within a world
Whose metes and bounds so narrow seem to
  us ;
Say, dost thou live and still enjoy thy fare
Of hemp and earth-brewed ale, with but a bone
From some poor fish on which to whet thy
  bill ?
While out of doors thy winged sisters glide
On supple wing, through fields and meadows
  fair
With blooming flora in its varied forms,
Through country, town, or great metropolis ;
Through grove and dale, or perched on the
  bough
Of genial tree or shrub, to catch their prey,
Or warble forth a descant to the winds ?
Say, art thou happy in thy solitude,
With naught but puny house-plant underneath
For contrast with the wainscot, sill, or wall ;

And bulky plaster canopy above,
To hide from view God's fair external shroud?

Art thou content to thus remain in-doors
In pent-up cell, exempt from Nature's bounds
Of infinite glory ; and suffice with view
Of landscape through the panes of lucid glass ;
While at thy side in beauteous brotherhood,
Thy winged mate in similar grievance hangs
Suspended with his cage, from lengths of
    wire?

So this thy lot has fate destined to be,
A prisoner yet unknown to freedom's will.
Farewell, oh, lovely bird, oh, type of love !
Continue in thy praise of Joy divine.
And when the shades of evening softly steal
O'er cot and vale, may rest thy eyelids seek ;
And when beneath thy wing thy head is laid
" May peace be with thee," is my silent prayer.
May thine be pleasant dreams 'til morning
    sun
Sheds forth his welcome rays o'er eastern hills.
Farewell ! Farewell !

    March, 1895.

THE BIRD'S OBITUARY.

Sequel to "To a Bird in a Cage."

Oh, innocence! My innocence!
   That thou shouldst meet thy fate
In this cruel manner, sad to tell,
   Oh, why should I relate?

Sweet freedom's air meant death to thee,
   I heard thy requiem sigh
Through grass and limb, I knew't meant death,
   'Twas in the feline eye.

I saw the death-trap opened wide;
   I saw thee in the tree;
A glance soon caught thy downward flight;
   The worst was yet to be.

The stealthy cat,—blood-thirsty wretch,—
   Alert for this gay fare,
Sprang swiftly towards the charmed prey,
   Despite my threats and care.

29

The end had come.   The act was done,—
    A pace she quick flew o'er,
And darted underneath the manse,
    My pet was seen no more.

Oh, pretty bird!   Oh, lovely bird!
    Thy song oft stirred my heart ;
Without thee life is not complete ;
    Why are we torn apart?

A bard doth love such noble forms
    As thee and thy sweet mates ;
Thy memory often moves his pen,
    And soul and mind inflates.

Thou wert content within thy cell ;
    No care of life had thee ;
But bush and tree proved danger's trap,
    Which thou wert wont to see.

Thy feathery coat, and corpulent crop !
    How dainty in the sight
Of crouching cat !—a leap, a bound,
    I scarce could trace his flight.

Say, wast thou conscious of the ire
  With which I whipped the thing
For this adroit carnal feat
  On thy soft breast and wing?

But why should I thus blame poor puss?
  'Tis instinct,—nothing more ;
As natural for a cat to kill
  As waves to dash on shore.

A man craves flesh and so does brute ;
  How closely they're allied !
'Tis flesh on flesh, and blood on blood,
  And both are satisfied.

But when one's pet is captured thus
  To serve a luxurious meal,
One's common sense is quick reversed,
  And wrath allowed to steal.

The cage (where thou wert caused to dwell)
  Hangs empty, silent, still ;
No more sweet notes pour gayly forth
  In mingled, transient trill.

No more I hear thy tender call ;
　No more thy rustling wing ;
I see thee not atilt on perch ;
　How strange thy mate doth sing !

The cage hangs empty,—thou art gone,
　And lonely is thy mate ;
And when I'm moved to write these lines,
　How can I hesitate ?

I loved thee, but I loved too well ;
　Fate cut in twain the tie ;
Thy memory'll ever leave a trace ;
　Recurring, leave a sigh.

　April, 1895.

SONNET.

To an Unknown Friend.

NOTE.—These lines were inspired by a spontaneous friendship arising through poems of a contemporary, occurring occasionally in *The Detroit Journal* as specimens of Michigan verse.—AUTHOR.

WHAT noble friendships from vague sources
    spring !
What unions brief epistles often bring ;
What ties may often bind a kindred heart
With one of likeness, although far apart !
And, if the winged poesy has inspired
A union thus (as I have so desired),
Then God ordain, for we are satisfied,
And God forbid that such can be denied.
Our faces are, as yet, unknown to each ;
But hearts.—We trust, no skill of man can teach
A dearer language than the human breast,
At once the giver and the thing carest ;

At once the thing that finds us here on earth ;
And, too, the secret of our heavenly birth.*

---

* If a man is of a kindly and loving nature, in sympathy with his kind, extending it to those about him and
around him, and respecting that which is right and just,
he is said to be "good-hearted," a term expressive of a
quality of the human breast, which, in reality, is a
property of the intellect. "The secret of our heavenly
birth" implies that one of this sort is welcome in the
sight of God.

TRUTH.*

Nature! How vast her bounds, and peerless
    Truth
The solvent of her problems all, —aye, Truth !
It stands alone, search as we may and long,
For likeness in the labyrinthine cells
Of Nature's most remote and obscure halls.
'Tis not as rock,—geology tells us no,—
For e'en the concrete silica must yield
Before the potent agencies of flame,
And veer from compact clod to molten stream.
Unlike the diamond? Yes, for e'en this gem,
This piece of adamant, is but a fraud,
But evanescence—that is all—compressed
By some strange law of Nature long ago.

------

* Truth is my religion. Truth, in my opinion, is the search-light of all the investigations of science. That is what we are striving for ; let us search for it in the life-book of Nature ; in the vast resources of the earth and air.—Author.

A fraud, I say, because when 'neath the spell
Of an electric, the scintillations cease,
And it becomes a tintless vapor.   Nay,
Not like the gem in this respect is Truth,
But, oh, how similar in brilliancy !
Yea, e'en surpasses it.   This is not all
(How different and yet how similar are the
        two !)
The diamond is a stranger to some men,
And so is Truth ; to some there is a veil,
The veil of unostentation one ; the screen
Of Truth, one placed there by the faltering
        hand
Of Error, Error !   Who can this deny?
This cruel, fallacious sophiste.   Oh, that she
Might be forever banished from men's sight,
And her dim and wavering beacon on the
        sands
And shoals in life's great, heaving sea, de-
        stroyed.
Nevermore to conjure innocent souls.
O Fate ! destroy her signal ; build a new,
And found it on a rock which will never fall.
May't be Truth's brilliant cresset ; may its rays,
United, shine, enlightening shore to shore.

TO A RAINBOW.

How fair thy form
As o'er the distant sky thou blendest !
And sending far thy mighty arm,
    In grace thou bendest.

How fair to sight,
As to thy vap'rous vault above
The skylark, fearless of his flight,
    Swiftly doth move !

How doth he sail,
This pilgrim of the air ! This form
Emblazoned on the ephemerous veil,—
    The fading swarm

Of silvery clouds,
Now dying with declining day,
Wrapped in the invisible shroud
    Of sheer decay !

Vainly the brush
Might rudely trace thee on the board,
But skill e'er fails; and thou dost crush
As doth the sword

Man's feeble power;
And thou dost steal away his charm; *
But thou dost sympathy embower,
And guide his arm.

Thou givest him thoughts,
But roughly dons the paint, and coarse
The workmanship. No softness fraughts,
As in thy force.

Alas, farewell!
Already dost thou fade, and leavest
Thy loved companion,† yet farewell.
Thy memory cleavest.

July 19, 1895.

---

* It irresistibly wins our admiration by the remarkable softness of its tone, thereby lessening the charm of the bow of the artist; but it gives to the latter an inspiration and prompts him to his best, which is but rude and rough in comparison.

† The rainbow being double, on the disappearance of one part the other is left alone.

EPISTLE TO A DEAR FRIEND.

Lines on the Departure of my Friend and Tutor,
A. E. Wilber.

So friends must part?
But fate must have his way.   We have been
     friends,
Yes, truest friends, indeed.   The tie that
     bound
Our sympathies and love has ne'er been cut in
     twain,
And God forbid that such may ever be.
Not by thy hand (?), surely not by mine,
Will it be severed, well we know ourselves,
But, needs be such the case, by one un-
     known.

What bond more sacred than sweet Friend-
     ship's tie !
What grief more heartfelt than the parting
     sigh !

What deep regret in soul-made farewell tears
Of hopeful youth or wiser elder years !
The suffering and the sorrow of the soul ;
The trespassing, the death-bed, and the goal !
All these are represented on the stage
Of life, and stamped on Fate's mysterious
        page.
Yea, all mankind must harbor such as these,
Despite gay thoughts of comfort, joy, and
        ease.
The poor, the rich, the meek, the proud, the
        brave ;
The workman, monarch, Christian, fop, the
        grave ;
The fool, the vagabond, and vagrant thief ;
The genius, artist, bard, and social chief ;
The pensive, clever, florid, and secure,—
Yea, all of these, and yet how many more !

So comes the tide when we must say fare-
        well.
Aye, sad, indeed, the word, like vesper bell
When good Apollo lays himself to rest,
Comes breathing on mine ear and stirs my
        breast.

Farewell? Ah! darkling comes that parting
    word,
Borne not on tinted wings of tell-tale bird,
But on thy own, thy own, thy faltering lips.
Its hungered burthen of my spirit sips.
Farewell! for soon we lisp and drift apart,
And each leave golden memories on each
    heart.
We trust 'tis not forever; nay, much less;
But may omnipotent Fate our union bless.
And with his wand, when thou art gone away,
With many a pass and indivisible stay,
This bond of friendship! may he bind it
    strong!
All this, I trust, he'll do, and not do wrong.

So thou dost go? May joy be ever thine,
And in Minerva's lap may thou recline.
May Wisdom's crest, beset with adamant,
Thy future efforts crown,—may naught sup-
    plant,—
And like the unseen power above, that guides
Man's feeble hand and stirs the ponderous
    tides

Of destiny, thy footsteps may she note,
And thus divert thee from the treacherous
    moat.*

---

* Man is a scheming genius.   Scheming is all right in
its place,—if we scheme to a good purpose, if the results
are going to benefit mankind.   But there are too many in
this world who, in their scheming after wealth and fame,
even resort to falsehood, and thus sometimes get a fellow-
creature "in a boat," to use the colloquial phrase.   A
man who thinks he is moving in the right path may be led
to his downfall by the *ignis fatuus* of some treacherous
speculator.   Therefore he must be on guard.—AUTHOR.

ODE TO THE SOUTH WIND.*

Thou unseen zephyr from some distant clime,
  Bowed down with fragrance from thy
    mother's breast,
Frolicking with Aurora in her prime,
  And kissing the earth, which thou hast oft
    carest ;
  Whither dost thou go?   Where's thy re-
    treat,—thy nest?

Art thou from heaven? Wast thou born of God?
  Has thy soft feet e'er trod those glittering
    spheres?
Or is earth thy mother? forever hast thou trod
  O'er the inglorious plain where heaven ne'er
    appears?
  This universal death-bed and this vale of
    tears.

---

* This " Ode" was suggested by the hopeful, inspiring
zephyrs of glorious May.   To the author it is even
passionate, and I do not feel satisfied until I have sung
its praise.

But hence. Sweet zephyr, come dispel such
    cares.
  Bring joy with thee ; vain sorrow must de-
    part,
For flowers appear despite a field of tares,
  And thus leave gems with which to cheer
    the heart.
  Thou unseen zephyr, come, disperse such
    cares athwart.

Welcome, sweet zephyr, from thy couch above,
  The breath of heaven moves thy immortal
    wings ;
Thou art the image of God's fearful love,
  As are the lords the breath of potent kings ;
  The eternal goddess fair, admonishing
    heavenly things.

Thou hast a message from Apollo's breast,
  And to the mother nature dost thou move
To bear its burthen to her teeming crest ;
  And so bring forth her smiles as those
    above,
  Inflate her soul with thine, and fill her with
    thy love.

The vigorous trees thou hast inspired with
    song,
And ever, in their own monotonous lay,
They murmur to themselves and to the throng
    That plods along the well-worn public way,
    Till good Apollo bids farewell to parting
    day.

E'en as the songsters poureth in full heart,
    Gay strains of love upon a tired earth,
To charm with all the skill of unlearned art,
    And soothe dull care with praise of graceful
    mirth ;
    We feel thou art its theme,—the prompter
    of his birth.

May, 1895.

GOD.

"Oh thou Eternal One!"
Thy mighty presence here,
Although unseen among
Us, brings to us the thoughts
Of master intellect
In realms beyond the grave;
Thoughts of the maker
Of this universe;
Thoughts of the one who guides
The ships through trackless depths
Thoughts of the one who stirs
    The tides of destiny;
And guides man's hand, and thus
Inspires the frailty of
His feeble intellect;
And fills his hung'ring soul
With love and light; and gives
Him power to raise mankind
To higher levels in
The silver spheres of Truth:

Thoughts of the one who gives
Life unto earth, and fills
The heart of nature full
With animation ; prompts
Her beings on life's path
To strive for higher things
Than earthly goals. We feel
Thy presence in the wood,
The stream, and depths of air.
And as we move at morn
Or evening to the haunts
In shady forest hearts ;
Or to her blest resorts,—
The caves in deep-delved earth,—
Apart from care and strife
Of routine worlds, to seek
Communion with her forms,
And solve her mysteries ;
We feel thy breath,
Thy presence, and thy love,
Thy whisper all around
That lisps thy truths, and binds
Our hearts to thee. Thou bring'st
To us the thoughts of this
Vast universe ; and lead'st

Our fancy's children through
The lapse of ages to
The birth of worlds ; and through
Immeasurable space beyond
The bounds of imagery,
Till we feel thy power,
And realize our own
Inferiority.
O God ! we feel thou art
In everything.
                    Thou com'st
To us in grief ; and thou
Dost send thy spirits (parts
Of Thee) to minister
Unto our woes till healed
By thy blest curative.
Teach us to live, that, when
Run down by death, our souls
May find a resting-place
In those eternal spheres
Thou hast prepared.   To go
To be a part of thee,
And with thee seek new truths,
And act thy laws for aye.

FOREST REVERIE.*

July 18—August 6.

"There is a pleasure in the pathless wood,
  There is a rapture on the lonely shore,
  There is society where none intrude,
  By the deep sea, and music in its roar.
  I love not man the less, but Nature more,
  From these our interviews, in which I steal
  From all I may be, or have been before,
  To mingle with the universe, and feel
What I can ne'er express, yet cannot all conceal."
                                            —BYRON.

HERE will I sit in this dim wood, and list
Unto the merry notes that greet mine ear ;
Notes of the songsters, in such gurgling glee
That songs become a liquid melody,
And flow, like silver streams, adown the sky.

---

* This poem was suggested and composed, in part, during one of my solitary rambles through the wood. The surroundings were remarkably striking, and so prompted me to write, and "Forest Reverie" is the product. It is an exact portraiture of the scene, with the exception of the cot described in the course of the poem, which is thoroughly imaginary.—AUTHOR.

Huge trees send up their growth, and pierce
    the vault
Of God's vast canopy, and hide the rays
Of that orbed flambeau,—shading me here,
    and thus
Making my sojourn sweet and free from care.
Now steals the breeze, which finds its welcome
    way
To my delightful resting-place upon
This venerable log, felled by some laboring
    swain
Long, long ago ; for mouldering now it lies
Deep in decay, surrendering up its growth
Unto the elements.   Ah ! such is life.
Man comes into the world, exists a time,
Then by the inevitable Death is stricken down,
To moulder in the sands.   There let him
    rest,
But speed his soul to fairer climes than ours !
Hard by, the placid stream, kissed by the
    breeze,
Hastens to greet its guest, then ripples on
O'er stones and crags, and through its winding
    path,
Beset with verdure.   Many a rustic bridge

Doth span the course, but sometimes rudely
  thrown
Into its bed, to check its favorite course.
But hasten on, thou child of earth and air,
And cease not till thou reach'st thy destiny.

My God is here. (The wood was God's first
  shrine.)
The trees attest His presence, and the wind
Breathes out to me a message of His love.

Say, what is this that I doth now discern
Far in the distant maze, surrounded by
The wood, and so made indistinct
By stalwart trunks, which intercept the range
Of vision. Now the sturdy oak in majesty
Doth rise and mock me fearlessly and bold.
The beech, birch, maple, each in turn appear
To serve that end, and last the spreading elm
Steals into view ; then, sending itself abroad,
It forms a vast corona,—strives to hide
The cot beneath, but strives and strives in
  vain.
I now advance, and slowly through the depths
Of trackless forestry doth stir my feet ;

Slowly and carefully, as did the child
Of Christ along the rugged mountain-path
When searching for the "end" in Christian
    life.*
Onward I press, and soon the enchanting bower
Receives my wearied form and gives me rest.
The ruined walk, the great elm-tree above,
The universe of wood, the flowery dale,
The grasses and the ivy creeping o'er
The crumbling wall, and o'er the tottering
    thatch,
Afford a pleasing scene and noble † thoughts.
I rest secure, as, casting a thoughtful glance,

---

* An allusion to Christian in Bunyan's "Pilgrim's Progress."

† It was first suggested to my mind to place "idle" here, but I did not wish to convey this to my readers.   It is a wrong idea.   I did not proceed to the wood to waste the time in idleness, but for thought ; to pamper the soul with the lessons and truths of our beneficent mother. Some people have the opinion that one is "lazy" if he does not employ himself in hard, manual labor.   Study and thought are considered idleness   But this we know is simply the height of ignorance.   These are the sentiments of people who do not think, and are not to' be considered by thinking people.—AUTHOR.

The sight soon falls upon the countless leaves.
Attached, I pause awhile, then murmur thus,—
" The leaves were born last spring, but to
    decay
The zephyrs now doth kiss them wantonly ;
Full soon November turns their shroud to gold,
And icy winter covers them with snow.
O Winter ! Why dost thou come here ?
On thy approach in this our northern home
I sooth would part with thee for fairer climes,
Where queenly Summer ever reigns supreme,
And o'er the teeming earth her mantle throws.
But here the lot forbids me to remain.*
Give me the live metropolis of the north,
The thriving town, and genial farms around.
Though cold the blast and chill the atmosphere,
'Tis past in time, and June again returns ;
The birds, the trees, the meadows then appear,
Our mother, Nature, smiles, then dons her best."
Now, strolling from the leaves to other sights,

---

* The climate of the torrid zone has a natural tendency
to produce unthriftiness. Life seems to be sluggish.
There is not the thrift here that occurs in the north.—
AUTHOR.

My thoughts run backward through the lapse
    of time
To when this wood was wrought with God's
    own hand ;
How, long ago, those cliffs of iceland* sought
To strew the land with rustic terraces ;
To leave their traces in the rising hills.
Here the warm sun sent forth his torrid rays
And bade the pompous heights yield at his will.
So yielded thus the cliffs of adamant ;
Thus caused a raging sea o'er all our land.

---

* Reference to the Glacial Period.   Steele, in a treatise
on the Glacial Epoch, carries our fancy so far in the fol-
lowing lines that we imagine we are gazing on the scene
itself :

"The valleys are filled with broad, deep, majestic
rivers, whose waters, flowing to the sea, dig deep chan-
nels, open new routes to the ocean, plough through moun-
tain ridges, sort and sift the drift *débris*, arranging it in
layers and forming alluvial deposits of a great thickness.
In many parts of the Northern States only the loftiest
mountains emerge above the engulfing waters.   Billows
roll where birds sang and flowers bloomed.   The land
gained during all these ages of geological history seems
lost again.   The ocean triumphs, and once more the Gulf
joins its waters with the Arctic Ocean."

Majestic streams gushed forth, and through
    the vale
The darkling waters rolled their billows high.
Here, where I sit, huge monsters of the deep
Once grovelled in the sands where rest my feet.
Here once the mammoth and the mastodon
Roamed through the wild with undivided sway;
The cave-bear slyly trod in quest of food.
But all are fled ; yes, all are buried now
Far in the deep-delved earth,—their clods as
    rock.
The soil on which I rest is not the soil
Which then received their footprints,—Father
    Time
Has placed a strata 'twixt their bones and me
Which ne'er shall be removed unless, per-
    chance,
Some dire convulsion of the Stygian hells
Shall rend its concrete structure to the winds.
Ah ! such has been the case when into form
God moulded first the plastic crust to grace
A sphere of life.   Three kingdoms * then up-
    rose,

---

* The mineral, vegetable, and animal kingdoms.

And soon a fourth,—the heavenly kingdom
    'twas.
And what is Life? 'Tis but a stage on which
We all are actors, but a play to please
The sight of Him who made it to destroy.
Orders and kingdoms rise and fall with laws
Of evolution and environments.
We learn through Science many laws of God,—
How first, from certain vap'rous elements,
A single cell is formed by synthesis,
Then, being nurtured by apt elements,
At last is graced an insect, flower, or man.
Thus through the ages beings lived and died,
Each giving place in turn to higher forms,
And lastly man. Here the rude savage
    roamed,
And once possessed the pleasure of the wood.
The deer, the elk, the bear fell at his will.
But he is gone, oppressed by English blood.
Where were his blest retreats not long ago
The crowded city mocks his useless toil ;
Great breadths of masonry obscure the spot
Where once he sat in council, as the flash
Of war rushed through his poor yet active
    brain.

Oh, blest the change! And honor to the men
Who dared to brave the perils of the deep,
Who dared to face the red-skin's poison dart,
Who civilized our far-famed hemisphere,
Who made the atrocious copper to submit.
Oh, noble fathers of America,
Thou gav'st to us our freedom and our tongue.
How can we thank thee other than by use
Of these, the boons which thou hast granted
    us?
America, our home, we reverence thee.
The vaulted roofs of heaven roll the sound
Of anthems back to greet our patriot hearts.
Thy fame transcends the glory of the east
When morning first ascends the golden sky,
When first she unfolds her robes and sends a
    flood
Of light to wake the slumbering maidens fair.
What lusty statesmen hast thou wrought!
    What wealth,
What wisdom, what prosperity thou hast!
But, oh, what vice! Canst thou not compre-
    hend?
Canst thou not fling this monster from thy
    bounds?

Canst thou not soon efface his tarnished name?
Oh, why dost thou remain, Illiteracy,
To rob the nation and its tender youth?
Art thou so stupid none can teach thee, say?
Get hence ; we care not for thy company.
But, Wisdom, come ; proclaim thy presence
     here ;
We'll sing thy praise in many a musèd rhyme.
Let Ignorance be bound with manly steel,
And cast her worthless body to the past.
The past! 'Tis gone ; nor could we wish it
     back.
The future's in our sight, and lo, behold!
The superior light shines indistinct before.

I watch the merry birds dart to and fro
From bough to bough, contented and in peace.
Let none disturb their fare.   But as they move
At evening to the streets, "the fowler's eye"
Detects their presence ; then his skill pours out
Their life-blood o'er a God-created breast.
Has man a heart?   If so, 'tis but a stone
When its true language tells the soul to kill.
Does he "ne'er think what wondrous beings
     these"?

Does he "ne'er think who made them and
    who taught
The dialect they speak"?   Man has a soul,
But 'tis a brute's when 't fells an innocent bird.

A wandering sunbeam comes to tell to me
That 'tis the hour of noon ; but where's my
    food?
I look in vain about me.   Pleasant the cot,
Pleasant this flowery nest, but not to starve.*
"If solitude makes scant the means of life,"
Our souls must seek a sustenance elsewhere.
Hence I will hie me homeward to my lodge.
The wood is rude,†—exempt from public strife,
From clanging hammers and the roar of
    wheels.
God's pristine handiwork stands undisturbed,‡
The same keen charm now marks it as of yore.
Man clears the forest, but the stroke forbade,
Which strikes the shrine from off the smiling
    earth.

---

* Meaning, not pleasant to starve.
† But is omitted here.
‡ The wood still stands in places with the same charm
and wildness as in earlier times.

Give me the city, but let not the wood
Be stricken from our clods' indulgences.
Yet, oh, for the city's walls, its burnished
 wealth,
Its culture, and its high society.
Here wisdom thrives, but we would ask for
 more.
Welcome the time when we'll no longer place
Upon the tombstone of some mouldering
 youth,—
"Fair Science frowned not on his humble
 birth."
"My visit still, but never my abode,"
The cot has left its trace upon the soul.

TO HER MATERNAL GRACE.

How oft in childhood's dark and weary hours
Has thy soft hand been laid upon my brow.
It seemed as if with supernatural power
To comfort me, and sympathy embower.
No balm, however sweet, can be compared
With this one. Nay, 't absconds into the depths
      Of sheer defeat.
A loss of thee can never be repaired.

THE END.

www.ingramcontent.com/pod-product-compliance
Lightning Source LLC
Chambersburg PA
CBHW021642270326
41931CB00008B/1123

* 9 7 8 3 3 3 7 3 2 9 1 7 4 *